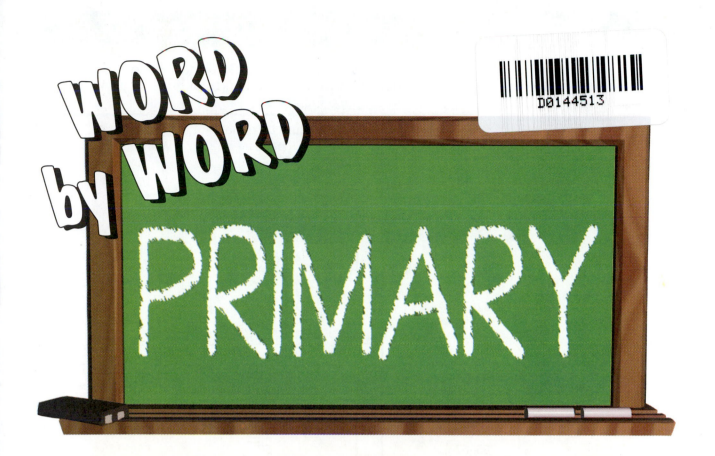

WORD by WORD

PRIMARY

LEVEL A PHONICS WORKBOOK

Steven J. Molinsky • Bill Bliss

Illustrated by

Richard E. Hill

Longman

Picture Dictionary / Level A Workbook Correlation

This correlation indicates the Word by Word Primary Phonics Picture Dictionary lessons designed for use at Level A and the correlated activity pages located in this workbook.

Picture Dictionary pages	Level A Workbook pages	Picture Dictionary pages	Level A Workbook pages
6	1	34	99–101
8	2–5	35	102–104
9	6–9	36	105–108
10	10–13	37	109
11	14–17	38	110–111
12	18–21	39	112–113
13	22–25	40	114–115
14	26–31	41	116–117
15	32–35	42	118–119
16	36–39	43	120–121
17	40–43	44	122–123
18	44–47	45	124–125
19	48–51	46	126–127
20	52–55	47	128–129
21	56–61	48	130–131
22	62–64	49	132–133
23	65–67	50	134–135
24	68–70	51	136–137
25	71–73	52–55	138–139
26	74–77	56–57	140
27	78–80	58–59	141
28	81–83	60–62	142
29	84–86	74	143
30	87–89	80	143
31	90–92	180–181	144–145
32	93–95	182–183	146–147
33	96–98	184–185	148–149

Editorial Director: *Louise Jennewine*
Executive Editor: *Anne Stribling*
Director of Design and Production: *Rhea Banker*
Associate Director of Electronic Publishing:
  Aliza Greenblatt
Production/Editorial Design Manager: *Paul Belfanti*
Production Manager: *Ray Keating*
Senior Manufacturing Manager: *Patrice Fraccio*
Manufacturing Buyer: *Dave Dickey*
Electronic Production Editors, Page Compositors,
  Interior Designers: *Paula Williams, Wendy Wolf*
Cover Designer: *Merle Krumper*
Cover Artists: *Richard E. Hill, Carey Davies*
Scanners, Color Correctors: *Todd D. Ware,*
  Robert W. Handago
Production Assistant: *Robert Siek*
Manuscript Preparation Assistant: *Rose Ann Merrey*
Illustrations: *Richard E. Hill*

Word by Word Level A Phonics Workbook
© 2000 by PEARSON EDUCATION

Pearson Education, 10 Bank St.,
White Plains, NY 10606

ISBN 0-13-028919-1

Printed in the United States of America

10 9 8 7 6 5 4

CONTENTS

Concepts About Print	1
Consonants *m, v* + Word Family *an*	2
Recognizing Same Letters & Words	3
Writing Letters *Vv, Mm*	4
Writing & Reading Practice	5
Consonants *c, p* + Word Family *an*	6
Recognizing Same Letters & Words	7
Writing Letters *Cc, Pp*	8
Writing & Reading Practice	9
Consonants *m, c, b* + Word Family *at*	10
Recognizing Same Letters & Words	11
Writing Letters *Aa, Bb*	12
Writing & Reading Practice	13
Consonants *m, c, l* + Word Family *ap*	14
Recognizing Same Letters & Words	15
Writing Letters *Ll, Mm*	16
Writing & Reading Practice	17
Consonants *p, b, w* + Word Family *ig*	18
Recognizing Same Letters & Words	19
Writing Letters *Ii, Ww*	20
Writing & Reading Practice	21
Consonants *p, s, k* + Word Family *it*	22
Recognizing Same Letters & Words	23
Writing Letters *Kk, Ss*	24
Writing & Reading Practice	25
Consonants *d, r, z* + Word Family *ip*	26
Recognizing Same Letters & Words	27
Writing Letters *Dd, Rr*	28
Writing Letters *Zz* & Complete Words	29
Listening: Initial Sounds	30
Writing & Reading Practice	31
Consonants *p, w, f* + Word Family *in*	32
Recognizing Same Letters & Words	33
Writing Letters *Nn, Ff*	34
Writing & Reading Practice	35
Consonants *l, f, h* + Word Family *og*	36
Recognizing Same Letters & Words	37
Writing Letters *Oo, Hh*	38
Writing & Reading Practice	39
Consonants *c, p, h* + Word Family *ot*	40
Recognizing Same Letters & Words	41
Writing Letters *Tt* & Complete Words	42
Writing & Reading Practice	43
Consonants *m, h, t* + Word Family *en*	44
Recognizing Same Letters & Words	45
Writing Letters *Ee* & Complete Words	46
Writing & Reading Practice	47
Consonants *p, n, g* + Word Family *et*	48
Recognizing Same Letters & Words	49
Writing Letters *Gg* & Complete Words	50
Writing & Reading Practice	51
Consonants *b, r, s* + Word Family *un*	52
Recognizing Same Letters & Words	53
Writing Letters *Uu* & Complete Words	54
Writing & Reading Practice	55
Consonants *m, b, j* + Word Family *ug*	56
Recognizing Same Letters & Words	57
Writing Letters *Jj* & Complete Words	58
Writing & Reading Practice	59
Listening: Initial sounds	60
Listening: Final sounds	61
Short Vowel Word Family *an*	62
Listening: Initial Consonants + *an*	63
Writing & Reading Practice	64
Short Vowel Word Family *ap*	65
Listening: Initial Consonants + *ap*	66
Writing & Reading Practice	67
Short Vowel Word Family *at*	68
Listening: Initial Consonants + *at*	69
Writing & Reading Practice	70
Short Vowel Word Family *ad*	71
Listening: Initial Consonants + *ad*	72
Writing & Reading Practice	73
Short Vowel Word Families *ag, am*	74
Writing Letters *Yy* & Complete Words	75
Listening: Initial Consonants + *ag, am*	76
Writing & Reading Practice	77
Short Vowel Word Family *ig*	78
Listening: Initial Consonants + *ig*	79
Writing & Reading Practice	80

Recognizing Same Letters & Words	81	Listening: Consonant *j* + Short Vowels	121
Listening: Initial Consonants + *ip*	82	Consonant *r* + Short Vowels	122
Writing & Reading Practice	83	Listening: Consonant *r* + Short Vowels	123
Short Vowel Word Family *it*	84	Consonant *l* + Short Vowels	124
Listening: Initial Consonants + *it*	85	Listening: Consonant *l* + Short Vowels	125
Writing & Reading Practice	86	Consonant *b* + Short Vowels	126
Short Vowel Word Family *ot*	87	Listening: Consonant *b* + Short Vowels	127
Listening: Initial Consonants + *ot*	88	Consonant *p* + Short Vowels	128
Writing & Reading Practice	89	Listening: Consonant *p* + Short Vowels	129
Short Vowel Word Families *og, op*	90	Consonant *d* + Short Vowels	130
Listening: Initial Consonants + *og, op*	91	Listening: Consonant *d* + Short Vowels	131
Writing & Reading Practice	92	Consonant *t* + Short Vowels	132
Short Vowel Word Family *et*	93	Listening: Consonant *t* + Short Vowels	133
Listening: Initial Consonants + *et*	94	Consonant *g* + Short Vowels	134
Writing & Reading Practice	95	Listening: Consonant *g* + Short Vowels	135
Short Vowel Word Family *en*	96	Consonants *c, k* + Short Vowels	136
Listening: Initial Consonants + *en*	97	Listening: Consonants *c, k* + Short Vowels	137
Writing & Reading Practice	98	Short Vowels Review: Which Word Doesn't Belong?	138
Short Vowel Word Family *ug*	99	Consonants Review: Initial & Final Sounds	139
Listening: Initial Consonants + *ug*	100	Rhyming Words	140
Writing & Reading Practice	101	Changes in Words	142
Short Vowel Word Families *un, ut*	102	Writing Letters *Xx, Qq*	143
Listening: Initial Consonants + *un, ut*	103	Colors and Shapes: Identifying	144
Writing & Reading Practice	104	Colors and Shapes: Sorting and Classifying	145
Short Vowel Word Families *ub, up, ud*	105	Classroom Objects, Toys, and Clothing: Identifying	146
Listening: Initial Consonants + *ub, up, ud*	106	Classroom Objects, Toys, and Clothing: Sorting and Classifying	147
Writing & Reading Practice	107	Food: Identifying	148
Word Family Review: Which Word Doesn't Belong?	108	Food and Clothing: Sorting and Classifying	149
Listening: Initial Short Vowels	109	Check-Up Test	150
Consonant *m* + Short Vowels	110	Answer Key and Listening Scripts	152
Listening: Consonant *m* + Short Vowels	111	The Alphabet	155
Consonant *n* + Short Vowels	112	Workbook Activity Instructions Key	156
Listening: Consonant *n* + Short Vowels	113		
Consonant *f* + Short Vowels	114		
Listening: Consonant *f* + Short Vowels	115		
Consonant *s* + Short Vowels	116		
Listening: Consonant *s* + Short Vowels	117		
Consonant *h* + Short Vowels	118		
Listening: Consonant *h* + Short Vowels	119		
Consonant *j* + Short Vowels	120		

Note: The symbol ⟵ in this workbook indicates a word in the past tense.

m ⓥ m v

van (man)

- -

van man

M	M	V	M	A
a	a	m	v	a
V	A	V	M	V
m	v	m	m	a
v	a	m	v	v

van	man	van	man	van
VAN	VAN	MAN	MAN	VAN
man	van	in	man	man
MAN	MAN	VAN	MAN	VAN
van	van	van	man	in

V v

M m

m v

v a n

a n

a n

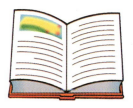

| van | man | man | van | van | man |
| a man in a van | | | a man in a van | | |

c   p   c   p

pan   can

pan   can

P	V	Ⓟ	Ⓟ	A
c	c	m	c	a
a	c	a	v	a
C	C	M	C	P
p	v	a	p	p

pan	(pan)	can	van	(pan)
can	man	can	can	pan
man	can	van	man	man
CAN	CAN	PAN	CAN	VAN
PAN	PAN	PAN	MAN	CAN

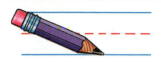

c p v

p a n

a n

a n

a n

can   pan   can   van   man   pan

a man and a can and a pan in a van

m (b) c   m b c   m b c

bat   can   (cat)

mat   bat   cat

can   man   mat

B	C	(B)	M	(B)
c	c	n	a	c
m	v	m	m	n
M	M	V	N	M
b	a	b	b	p

bat	(bat)	cat	(bat)	mat
CAT	CAN	CAT	CAT	BAT
mat	cat	bat	mat	mat
BAT	BAT	MAT	CAT	BAT
cat	cat	can	cat	mat

WRITING LETTERS *Aa, Bb*

DICTIONARY
page 10

A a

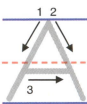

B b

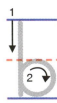

b c m

c a t

a t

a t

a t

cat   can   bat   pan   man   mat

a man and a cat and a bat in a van

m ⓒ l   m c l   m c l

   map   lap   cap

   lap   can   cap

   map   man   lap

14

c	l	ⓒ	ⓒ	a
L	V	L	M	L
m	m	c	a	m
l	l	b	p	l
C	P	B	C	C

CAP	LAP	(CAP)	(CAP)	MAP
lap	lap	bat	lap	pan
cap	pan	can	cap	cap
map	map	mat	map	man
LAP	CAP	LAP	PAN	LAP

Ll

Mm

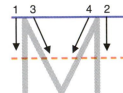

c m l

m a p

a p

a p

a p

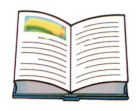

cap   can   map   man   van   lap

a map and a cap and a mat in a van

b p (w)   b p w   b p w

   lap   bat   (big)

   wig   map   pig

   big   pig   pan

W	(W)	V	(W)	A
i	l	i	i	t
w	m	w	v	w
I	I	L	I	L
W	M	V	W	W

wig	(wig)	pig	(wig)	big
BIG	PIG	BIG	BIG	BAT
big	big	pig	bat	big
PIG	PAN	BIG	PIG	PIG
pig	pig	big	pig	wig

Ii

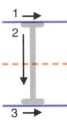

Ww

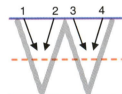

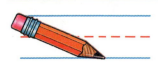

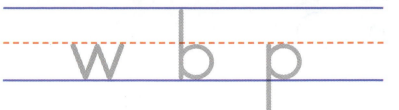

w b p

pig

ig

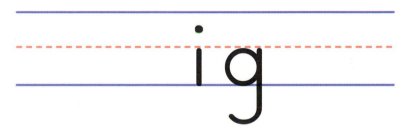

ig

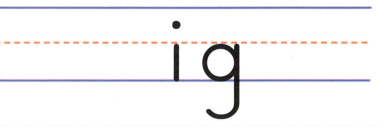

ig

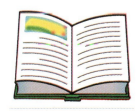

pig   pan   big   bat   wig   map

a pig and a cat in a big van

(k) p s   k p s   k p s

   pit   **(sit)**   kit

   cat   pit   kit

   pit   pan   sit

s	s	k	c	s
K	B	K	A	K
p	p	k	p	b
k	l	b	k	k
S	B	S	S	P

kit	sit	kit	kit	pit
SIT	SIT	BIG	SIT	KIT
pit	pig	big	pit	pit
KIT	KIT	KIT	PIT	SIT
sit	wig	sit	kit	sit

K k

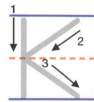

S s

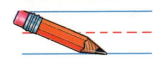

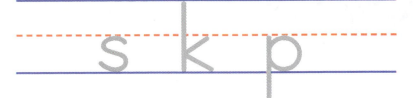

s k p

s i t

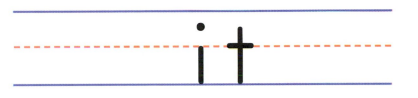

i t

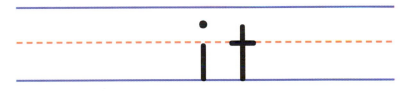

i t

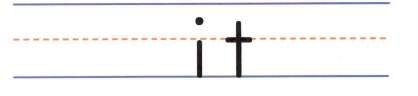

i t

pit   pig   kit   big   sit   wig

Sit on a big pig in a wig.

d (r) z   d r z   d r z

   sit   rip   (zip)

   kit   dip   rip

   zip   wig   rip

D	B	(D)	P	(D)
r	r	z	c	r
Z	V	Z	Z	A
R	R	P	R	B
d	b	p	d	d

rip	pig	zip	(rip)	(rip)
ZIP	ZIP	DIP	ZIP	RIP
dip	big	dip	pit	dip
RIP	RIP	RIP	PIT	ZIP
zip	zip	rip	zip	dip

Dd

Rr

WRITING LETTERS *Zz* & COMPLETE WORDS

DICTIONARY page 14

Z z

1 2 Z 3

1 2 z 3

zip

ZIP

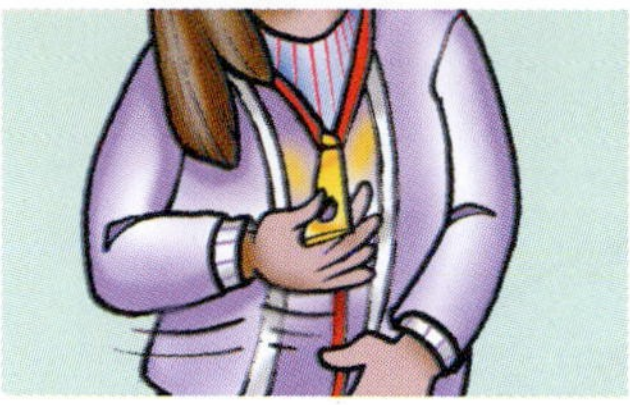

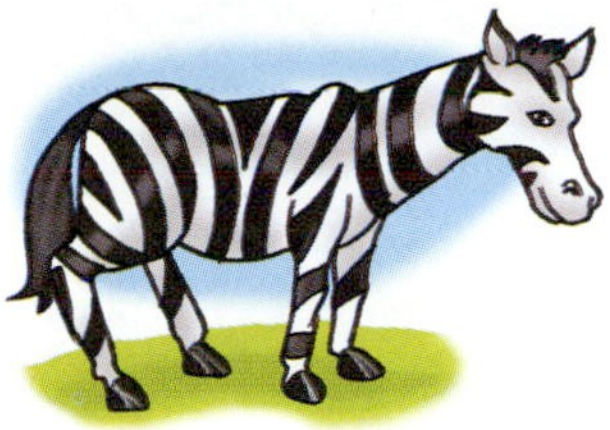

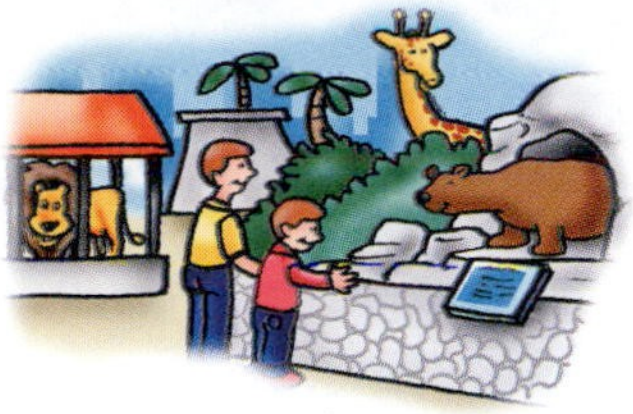

rip

1.

2.

3.

4.

5.

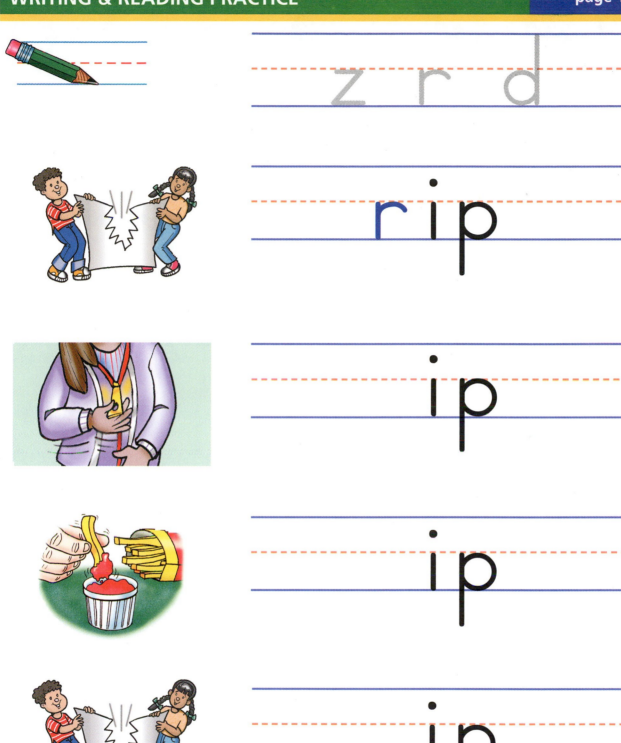

z r d

rip

ip

ip

ip

rip	pit	dip	big	zip	sit

A pig and a cat rip a cap.

 **w** f p   w f p   w f p

 pit   (pin)   fin

 fin   wig   win

 fin   pin   kit

F	B	(F)	K	(F)
f	f	k	b	f
N	N	V	N	M
w	m	w	n	w
n	m	n	n	w

win	(win)	pin	fin	(win)
PIN	PAN	PIN	PIG	PIN
fin	pin	win	fin	fin
WIN	WIN	WIN	FIN	PIN
pin	pit	pin	pan	pin

Nn

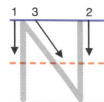

F f

w f p

fin

in

in

in

pin   pit   pig   win   wig   fin

Win a wig and a big pin with a fin.

l (f) h   l f h   l f h

   log   (hog)   fog

   fog   log   hog

   hog   lap   log

l	i	(l)	b	(l)
H	H	N	H	K
o	a	o	o	c
h	n	h	h	b
F	F	B	H	F

log	(log)	fog	hog	(log)
FOG	LOG	FOG	FOG	HOG
hog	hog	log	hog	fog
LOG	LAP	FOG	LOG	LOG
fog	log	fog	hog	fog

O o

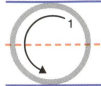

H h

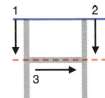

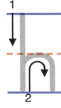

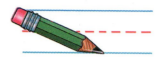

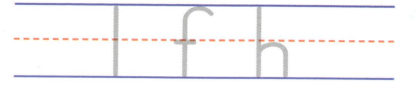

l f h

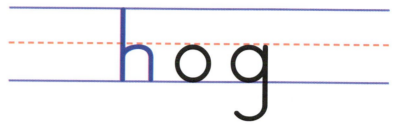

h o g

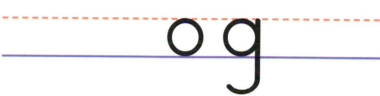

o g

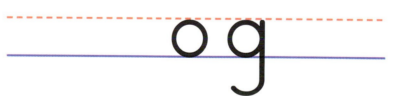

o g

o g

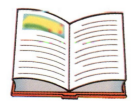

log   hog   fog   fin   lap   log

Sit with a hog on a log in the fog.

c h (p)   c h p   c h p

   (hot)   cot   hog

   cat   pot   cot

   pit   pot   hot

P	(P)	B	R	(P)
T	L	T	T	K
c	o	c	a	c
t	i	t	f	t
h	b	h	n	h

POT	(POT)	PIN	(POT)	HOT
hot	cot	hot	hog	hot
COT	COT	CAT	HOT	COT
pot	pit	pot	cot	pot
HOT	POT	COT	HOT	HOT

T t

pit

mat

cot

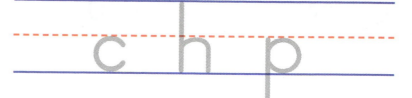

c h p

hot   hot

ot

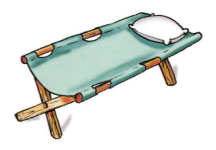

ot

ot

hot	hat	pit	pot	cat	cot

A hog and a cat sit on a cot.

m h (t)   m h t   m h t

men   ten   (hen)

hen   men   map

men   hot   ten

h	(h)	k	(h)	b
e	c	e	e	a
m	m	n	m	h
E	H	F	E	E
M	M	W	N	M

HEN	HOT	(HEN)	(HEN)	HOG
men	men	man	mat	men
TEN	HEN	TEN	MEN	TEN
MEN	MAN	MAP	MEN	MEN
ten	ten	hen	men	ten

E e

1 2

3

4

e

men

hen

ten

h m t

men   men

en

en

en

hen   hot   ten   map   men   man

A hen and a pig sit on a mat.

n p (g)   n p g   n p g

   get   pet   (net)

   pit   pot   pet

   hot   get   pet

n	m	(n)	(n)	h
p	p	b	p	d
G	C	G	O	G
N	N	M	V	N
g	p	g	b	g

net	(net)	get	pet	(net)
PET	POT	PET	PIT	PET
GET	COT	GET	GET	PET
get	get	pet	net	get
NET	NAT	GET	NET	NET

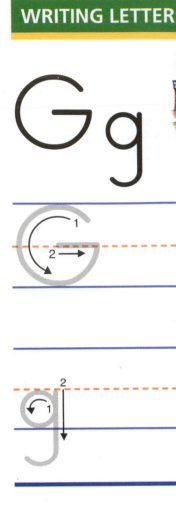

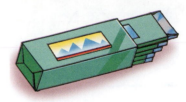

log

big

pig

n p g

net   net

et

et

et

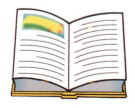

| pet | pit | get | pot | net | ten |

Ten men get a big net.

r (s) b   r   s   b   r   s   b

   (run)   sun   bun

   bat   big   bun

   sit   sun   run

R	R	P	R	B
s	z	s	s	r
U	U	V	W	U
b	d	b	p	b
u	n	u	v	u

RUN	PIN	RUN	BUN	RUN
SUN	SUN	RUN	BUN	SUN
bun	bat	big	bun	bun
run	sun	run	bun	run
BUN	BUN	RUN	SUN	BUN

U u

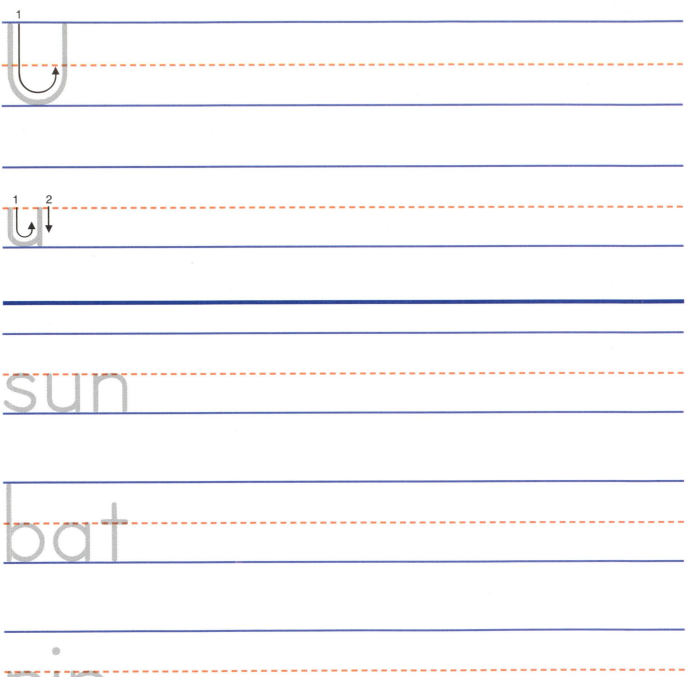

1

2

sun

bat

rip

r   s   b

run   run

un

un

un

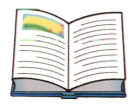

bun   bat   run   rip   sit   sun

A hen and a hog sit in the hot sun.

(m) b j   m b j   m b j

   big   (bug)   jug

   run   mat   mug

   get   jug   bug

56

G	C	(G)	O	(G)
J	J	T	F	J
g	g	p	g	d
j	g	j	p	j
m	n	r	m	m

MUG	BUG	(MUG)	(MUG)	JUG
bug	bun	jug	bug	bug
JUG	BUG	JUG	MUG	JUG
jug	mug	jug	jug	bug
mug	mug	run	jug	mug

Jj

j

j

jug

bun

map

m b j

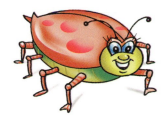

bug   bug

ug

ug

ug

bug   bun   mug   jug   big   bug

A jug and a pot sit in the hot sun.

1.

2.

3.

4.

5.

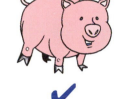

1. _____   ✔   **pig**

2. _____   _____   **ca**

3. _____   _____   **ma**

4. _____   _____   **bu**

5. _____   _____   **ho**

m (f) p   c r v   c t m   f p r

   fan   pan   (man)   tan

   van   ran   can   man

   ten   fan   pan   tan

   fin   fan   tan   man

1.   ✔   can

2.     an

3.     an

4.    an

5.     an

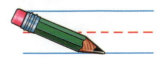

 fan
(pan)

pan

 man
ran

 can
van

 tan
can

 ran
van

fan   fin   run   ran   ten   tan

Dan and Jan ran in the hot sun.

n s (m) n g c c t l s l r

sap   gap   lap   (cap)

log   lap   tap   rap

map   nap   gap   tap

sap   cap   nap   rap

1.   ✔ ____   ____   s a p

2.   ____   ____   a p

3. ____    ____   a p

4. ____    ____   a p

5.   ____   ____   a p

cap
gap

sap
rap

map
nap

lap
sap

tap
rap

cap

rap   ran   cap   can   pan   nap

Get a cap and get a map.

67

DICTIONARY
page **24**

s (c) v   m n f   v b r   h v f

rat   fat   (bat)   mat

vat   hat   sat   cat

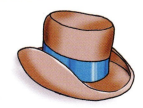

fat   sat   cat   mat

cat   mat   rat   sat

1.

_____ ✔

m a t

2.

_____ _____

a t

3.

_____ _____

a t

4.

_____ _____

a t

5.

_____ _____

a t

hat
(bat)

bat

cat
sat

fat
hat

fat
vat

rat
mat

cat   cap   can   map   man   mat

A cat and a rat sat on a big mat.

p   s   (b)   l   d   p   p   s   l   m   b   s

   (pad)   dad   sad   bad

   bad   sad   lad   mad

   sad   mad   pad   lad

   bad   mad   pad   sad

1.

sad

✔ _____   _____

2.

ad

_____   _____

3.

ad

_____   _____

4.

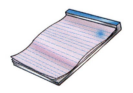

ad

_____   _____

5.

ad

_____   _____

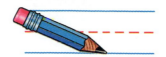

pad
dad

pad

mad
sad

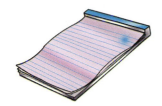

lad
mad

bad
pad

lad
dad

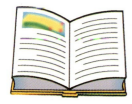

mad   mat   sad   sap   lap   lad

A sad lad sat on a lap.

h （w） r   b t j   r y h   y j t

 bag （tag） ham yam

 jam wag dam rag

 rag ham wag dam

 yam jam ham rag

74

ab

yam

yes

1. _____   ✔   bag

2. _____   _____   ag

3. _____   _____   ag

4. _____   _____   am

5. _____   _____   am

 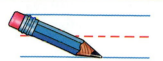 

rag
(wag)

wag

tag
rag

jam
yam

jam
ham

bag
dam

bag	bad	bat	tag	tap	jam

Get jam, ham, and a yam in a big bag.

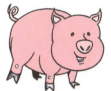   

(p) f b   b j d   b d f   r p j

   fig   pig   (big)   dig

   wig   rig   jig   pig

   big   dig   jig   rig

   wig   fig   big   jig

78

1.
 _____    ✔

big

2.
 _____    _____

ig

3.
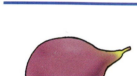 _____    _____

ig

4.
 _____    _____

ig

5.
 _____    _____

ig

 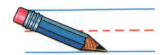

fig
(wig)

wig

dig
fig

big
rig

pig
dig

jig
rig

big   bag   rag   rig   wig   wag

A pig and a big cat dig and dig.

r （l） z   r   t   h   z   d   s   r   t   h

   （rip）   tip   lip   hip

   sip   dip   zip   rip

   hip   dip   lip   tip

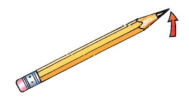   hip   sip   dip   tip

1. ✔ ___   ___  rip

2. ___   ___  ip

3. ___   ___  ip

4. ___   ___  ip

5. ___   ___ ip

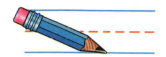

(lip)
zip

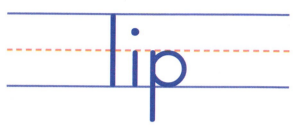

lip

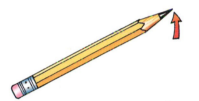

rip
sip

tip
zip

dip
rip

hip
dip

dip   dig   rip   rig   tag   tip

Rip a rag and dip it in a big vat.

f b (p)   k s z   l h b   f k h

   sit   pit   (fit)   lit

   kit   bit   hit   pit

   zit   bit   sit   lit

   fit   sit   hit   zit

1.   _____ ✔

2.   _____ _____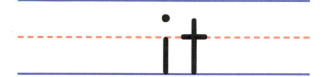

3. _____ _____

4.  _____ _____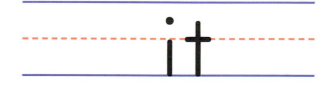

5.  _____ _____

 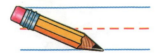

zit

(sit)

 sit

kit

lit

pit

lit

hit

fit

bit

zit

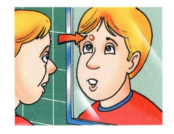

| bit | bat | hit | hot | sit | sat |

A bat hit a cat and bit a rat.

g (h) l   p t d   c g d   l p g

(cot)   tot   pot   hot

get   dot   tot   got

dot   pot   tot   hot

hog   hot   lot   cot

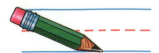

1.
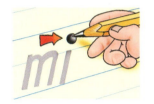

✔ _____   _____

dot

2.

_____   _____

ot

3.

_____   _____

ot

4.

_____   _____

ot

5.

_____   _____

ot

WRITING & READING PRACTICE

 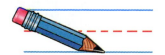

(got)
pot

got

hot
dot

lot
tot

dot
cot

tot
lot

| got | get | hot | hat | pot | pit |

A tot sat on a big cot.

b h (f)   m l t   h p m   h f b

   fog   log   (bog)   top

   hog   hop   mop   log

   tap   tip   pot   top

   mop   pop   top   hop

  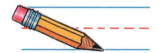

1.  _____  ✔  hog

2.  _____  _____  og

3.  _____  _____  og

4.  _____  _____ 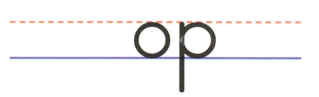 op

5.   _____  _____ op

bog
(fog)

fog

log
pop

hop
top

mop
hog

top
bog

bog   bag   big   tip   tap   top

Hop on a log in a big bog.

j （g） p   n s m   v w j   p w v

pit   pot   jet   （pet）

- -

jet   get   pet   met

- -

sit   sat   set   net

- -

net   met   pet   vet

1. ✔ _____   _____   get

2. _____   _____   et

3. _____   _____   et

4. _____   _____   et

5. _____   _____   et

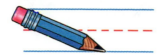

(pet)
get

pet

jet
get

set
jet

net
met

vet
wet

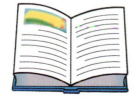

set   sat   get   got   pot   pet

The vet and the pet met on a jet.

(h) t d   m p h   m t d   p h t

ten   (pen)   Ben   men

men   ten   hen   den

den   Ken   hen   pen

men   pen   Len   ten

1.  _____  ✔

ten

2.  _____  _____

en

3.  _____  _____

en

4.  _____  _____

en

5.  _____ _____

en

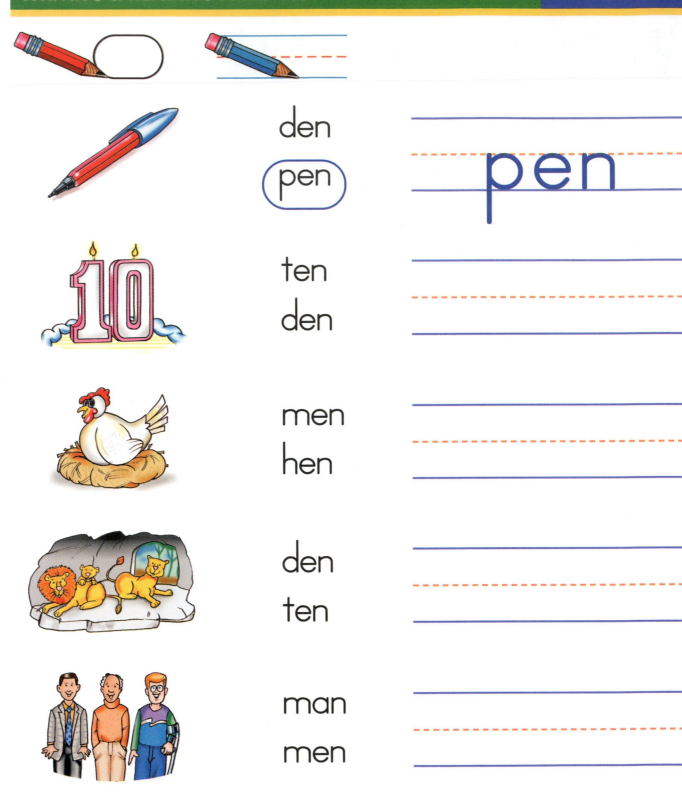

den
(pen)

pen

ten
den

men
hen

den
ten

man
men

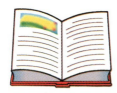

pin	pen	pan	tan	ten	men

A hen sat in a big den.

t (d) j   b t h   m j t   d r b

   dug   tug   (jug)   rug

   rug   bug   hug   dug

   mug   tug   bug   hug

   hug   bug   tug   dug

DICTIONARY
page 34

1. ___ ✔   ___

bug

2. ___   ___

ug

3. ___   ___

ug

4. ___   ___

ug

5. ___   ___

ug

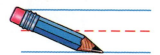

rug
mug

tug
hug

dug
bug

tug
jug

dug
jug

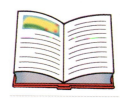

bug   bag   big   rag   rug   tug

A wet bug sat in a big jug.

(r) f b   c h s   s c n   h n r

 (fun)   sun   rut   hut

 run   nut   rut   bun

 fun   hut   cut   nut

 cut   sun   hut   rut

1. _____   ✔   s u n

2. _____   _____   u n

3. _____   _____   u t

4. _____   _____   u n

5. _____   _____   u t

sun
(run)

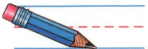 run

fun
bun

nut
hut

sun
cut

run
rut

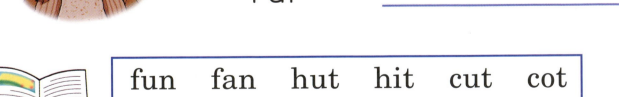

fun   fan   hut   hit   cut   cot

Get a hot bun and cut it.

s   c   (t)   r   s   c   c   p   b   m   r   b

tub   sub   (rub)   cub

cup   cub   pup   bud

sub   cup   bud   pup

mud   bud   rub   tub

1.  _____    ✔    rub

2.  _____    _____    ub

3.  _____    _____    up

4.  _____    _____    ub

5.  _____   _____    ud

(tub)
bud

tub

sub
cup

rub
bud

cub
cup

rub
pup

cub   cup   cap   bad   bud   bug

The cub and the pup sit in the mud.

  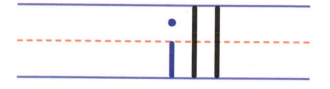

1. _____ _____ ✔

i l l

2. _____ _____

g g

3. _____ _____

d d

4. _____ _____

p

5. _____ _____

n

 ab

a e i o u

m a t   m   m   m   d

m   t   m   ll   m   p

mat	man	men	mop	mug	mill

Mud is on the mop and the mat.

1. ✔ ____ | ____ | mill

2. ____ | ____

3. ____ | ____

4. ____ | ____

5. ____ | ____

a e i o u

 n e t
 n t
 n p

 n d
n t
 n t

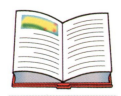

not   nut   nit   net   Nat   nap

The nit is not on the neck.

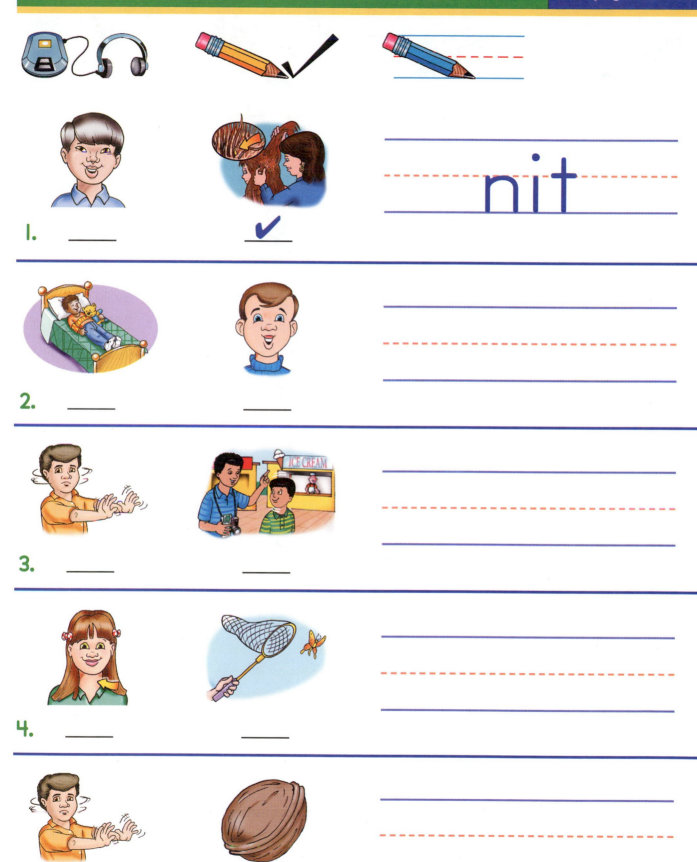

1. nit

2.

3.

4.

5.

 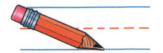ab

a   e   i   o   u

f in   f   g   f   n

f d   f   g   f   n

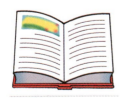

fan   fun   fin   fog   fig   fed

Nat fed the fat pig a big fig.

1. ✔ _____   _____   *fat*

2. _____   _____

3. _____   _____

4. _____   _____

5. _____   _____

a e i o u

 s n

sat s n s p

s b s t s d

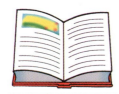

| sit | set | sat | sob | sub | sun |

Sit in the sub. Sit in the sun.

set

1. _____   ✔

2. _____   _____

3. _____   _____

4. _____   _____

5. _____   _____

 ab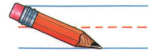

a e i o u

h**em**   h __ t   h __ g

h __ m   h __ n   h __ p

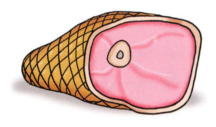

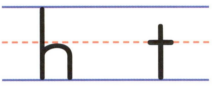

hut   hit   hat   hip   hop   hen

The hog and the hen hop in the hut.

1. _____   ✔

hip

2. _____   _____

3. _____   _____

4. _____   _____

5. _____   _____

 ab

a e i o u

jug   j_t   j_m

j_b   j_g   j_g

jig   jug   jog   Jack   jam   jet

Jeff and Jill sell jam to Jack.

1.   ✔ _____   _____   *Jill*

2.  _____   _____

3.   _____   _____

4.  _____   _____

5.   _____   _____

ab

a e i o u

rug   r t   r p

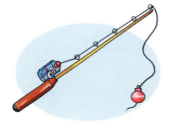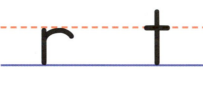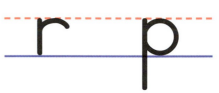

r d   r d   r n

rat   ran   rig   rug   red   rod

The red rod is on the rock.

122

1. _____   ✔ _____   rip

2. _____   _____

3. _____   _____

4. _____   _____

5. _____   _____

 ab

a e i o u

l og   l p   l g

l p   l d   l t

| lot | log | leg | led | lad | lap |

The lad led us to the lot.

log

1.  ✔ _____   _____

2.     _____   _____

3.     _____   _____

4.     _____   _____

5.  _____   _____

 ab

a e i o u

b a g   b _ s   b _ d

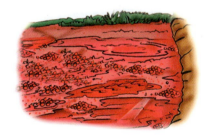

b _ b   b _ g   b _ t

| bug | bag | big | beg | bog | bus |

Bob is on the bus with a big bag.

bed

1. _____ ✔

2. _____ _____

3. _____ _____

4. _____ _____

5. _____ _____

 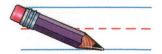

a e i o u

 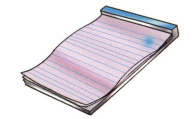 

p**en**   p   d   p   p

p   p   p   n   p   t

pen	pan	pin	pup	pop	pet

The pup sat with a pad and a pen.

128

1.

✔   pet

2.

3.

4.

5.

 ab

a e i o u

  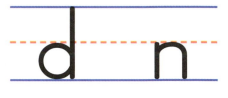

dig d m d n

d p d t d ck

| dig | dip | dot | dad | duck | den |

Dad is in the den with the duck.

1. ✔ _____   _____   dad

2. _____   _____

3. _____   _____

4. _____   _____

5. _____   _____

ab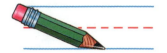

a   e   i   o   u

t u b   t   g   t   p

t   n   t   p   t   g

tip	top	ten	tan	tag	tug

Tell the tot the top is in the tub.

1. _____   ✔   *tag*

2. _____   _____

3. _____   _____

4. _____   _____

5. _____   _____

 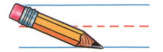

a e i o u

 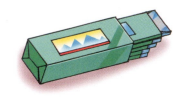 

g e t   g   m   g   s

g ll   g t   g p

get   got   gas   gull   gill   gap

Bob got gum and Jill got gas.

1.  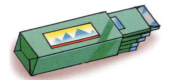 ✔ _____   _____   get

2.     _____   _____

3.     _____   _____

4.     _____   _____

5.  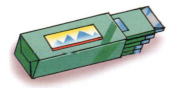   _____   _____

 ab

a e i o u

 cut  k d c  c d

 c t  c b  c t

cat   cut   kit   cot   can   Ken

Get the kit!   The cat got a cut!

1. can

(t) t   t (p)   (p) t  (t) p

p t   t p

t  t   t  t
n n   n n

s  s   s  s
b b   b b

p  p   p  p
n n   n n

m  m   m 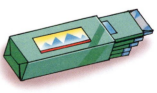 m
g g   g g

t  t   t  t
p p   p p

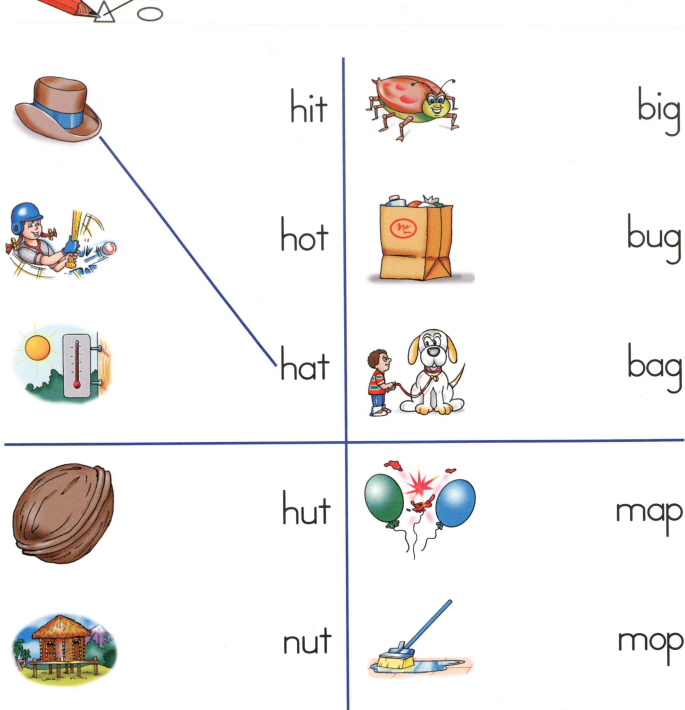

hit

big

hot

bug

hat

bag

hut

map

nut

mop

hug

pop

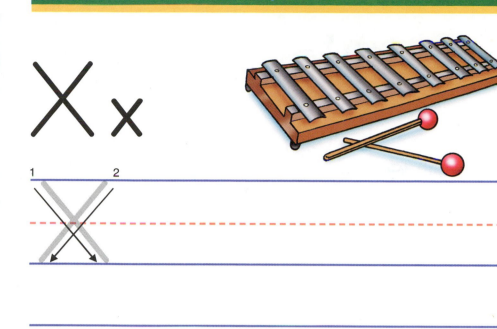

X x

1   2

1   2

Q q

1
2

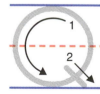

2
1

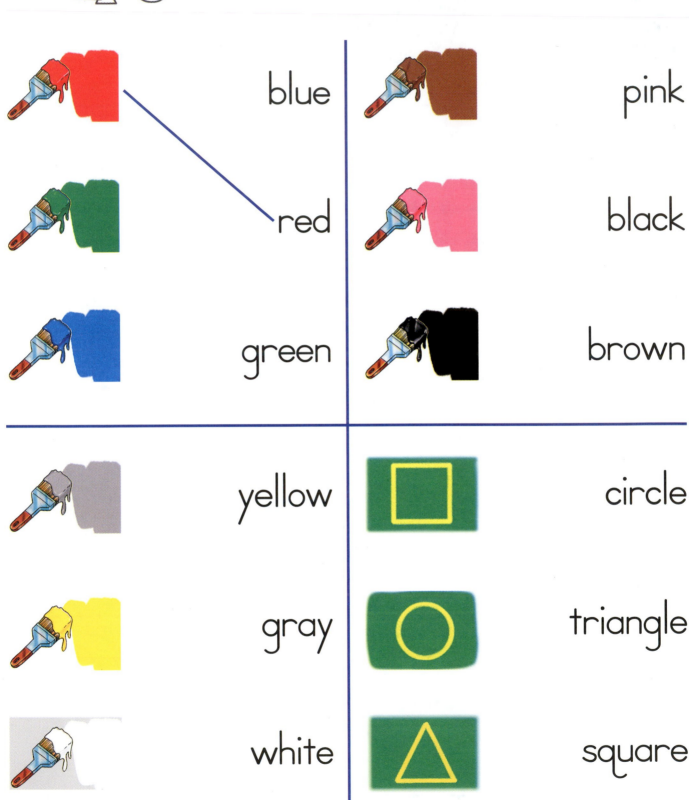

blue

red

green

yellow

gray

white

pink

black

brown

circle

triangle

square

 ? ?

black   circle   green   oval   pink   rectangle   red   square

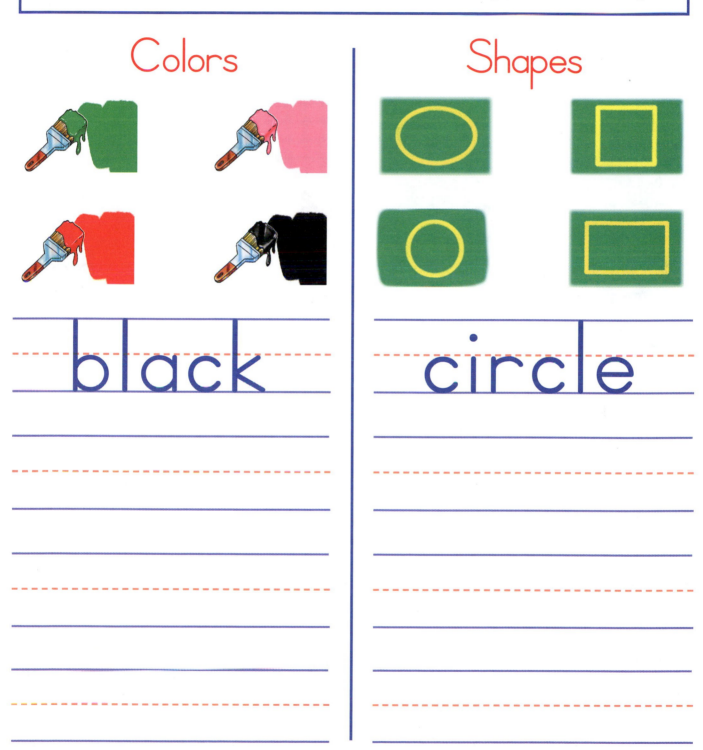

Colors

Shapes

black

circle

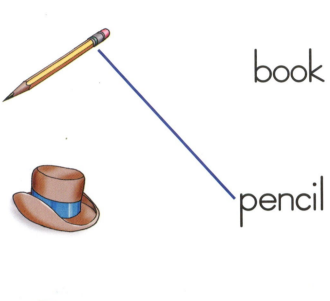

book

 skirt

pencil

 doll

hat

 globe

cap

 chair

crayon

 shirt

desk

 yo-yo

| book | cap | coat | desk | doll | dress | hat | yo-yo |

Objects & Toys

Clothing

book

cap

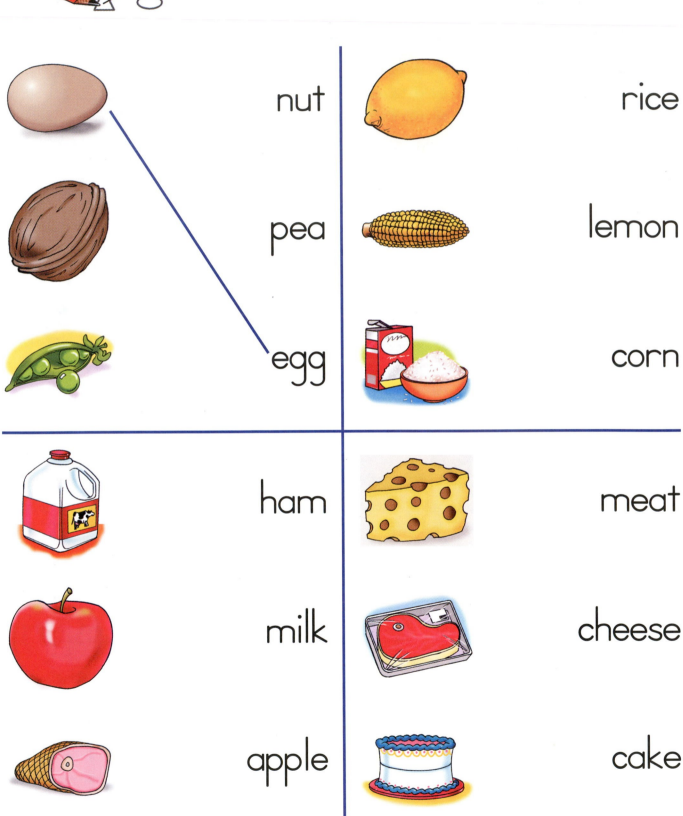

nut

pea

egg

rice

lemon

corn

ham

milk

apple

meat

cheese

cake

? ?

| boot | cake | cap | coat | fig | ham | hat | pea |

Clothing

Food

boot

a e i o u

mop pg jt

rn bg pt

tn sn mp

CHECK-UP TEST (PART 2)

log

1. _____ ✔

2. _____ _____

3. _____ _____

4. _____ _____

5. _____ _____

ANSWER KEY AND LISTENING SCRIPTS

PAGE 1
Students practice left-to-right and top-to-bottom progressions by tracing each line to connect the related pictures.

PAGE 2
v   m
man
van

PAGE 5
van
man
van

PAGE 6
p   c
pan
can

PAGE 9
pan
can
van
pan

PAGE 10
b   m   c
cat
bat
mat

PAGE 13
cat
mat
bat
cat

PAGE 14
c   l   m
lap
cap
map

PAGE 17
map
cap
lap
map

PAGE 18
w   b   p
big
wig
pig

PAGE 21
pig
wig
big
pig

PAGE 22
k   s   p
sit
kit
pit

PAGE 25
sit
kit
pit
sit

PAGE 26
r   d   z
zip
dip
rip

PAGE 30
Listen and choose the correct picture.
1. pit
2. zip
3. bat
4. cap
5. pig

PAGE 31
rip
zip
dip
rip

PAGE 32
w   p   f
pin
win
fin

PAGE 35
fin
pin
win
fin

PAGE 36
f   h   l
hog
fog
log

PAGE 39
hog
log
fog
hog

PAGE 40
p   h   c
hot
cot
pot

PAGE 43
hot
cot
pot
hot

PAGE 44
t   h   m
hen
men
ten

PAGE 47
men
ten
hen
men

PAGE 48
g   p   n
net
pet
get

PAGE 51
net
get
pet
net

PAGE 52
s   b   r
run
bun
sun

PAGE 55
run
sun
bun
run

PAGE 56
m   j   b
bug
mug
jug

PAGE 59
bug
mug
jug
bug

PAGE 60
Listen and choose the correct picture.
1. pin
2. get
3. jug
4. hen
5. fog

PAGE 61
Listen and choose the correct picture.
1. pig
2. can
3. map
4. bug
5. hot

PAGE 62
f   v   c   p
man
ran
tan
fan

PAGE 63
Listen and choose the correct picture.
1. can
2. tan
3. pan
4. ran
5. fan

PAGE 64
pan
man
van
can
ran

PAGE 65
m   n   t   r
cap
lap
gap
sap

PAGE 66
Listen and choose the correct picture.
1. sap
2. cap
3. lap
4. nap
5. gap

PAGE 67
cap
rap
map
sap
tap

PAGE 68
c   m   r   v
bat
hat
fat
sat

PAGE 69
Listen and choose the correct picture.
1. mat
2. rat
3. sat
4. bat
5. vat

PAGE 70
bat
cat
hat
fat
mat

PAGE 71
b   d   p   s
pad
lad
mad
sad

PAGE 72
Listen and choose the correct picture.
1. sad
2. mad
3. lad
4. pad
5. bad

PAGE 73
pad
sad
mad
bad
dad

PAGE 74
w   b   h   j
tag
rag
dam
yam

PAGE 76
Listen and choose the correct picture.
1. bag
2. tag
3. wag
4. ham
5. dam

PAGE 77
wag
rag
yam
jam
bag

PAGE 78
p   d   b   j
big
wig
rig
fig

PAGE 79
Listen and choose the correct picture.
1. big
2. rig
3. wig
4. fig
5. pig

PAGE 80
wig
fig
big
dig
jig

PAGE 81
l   r   s   h
rip
zip
dip
tip

PAGE 82
Listen and choose the correct picture.
1. rip
2. hip
3. zip
4. lip
5. sip

PAGE 83
lip
sip
tip
rip
dip

PAGE 84
p   s   l   h
fit
kit
bit
zit

PAGE 85
Listen and choose the correct picture.
1. fit
2. hit
3. lit
4. bit
5. sit

PAGE 86
sit
kit
pit
fit
zit

PAGE 87
h   p   d   l
cot
got
tot
hot

PAGE 88
Listen and choose the correct picture.
1. dot
2. lot
3. got
4. pot
5. cot

PAGE 89
got
hot
tot
dot
lot

PAGE 90
f   l   m   h
bog
hog
top
pop

PAGE 91
Listen and choose the correct picture.
1. hog
2. fog
3. bog
4. pop
5. mop

PAGE 92
fog
log
hop
hog
top

PAGE 93
g   n   w   v
pet
jet
set
met

PAGE 94
Listen and choose the correct picture.
1. get
2. set
3. pet
4. wet
5. met

PAGE 95
pet
get
jet
net
vet

PAGE 96
h   p   m   t
pen
hen
den
ten

PAGE 97
Listen and choose the correct picture.
1. ten
2. hen
3. den
4. men
5. pen

PAGE 98
pen
ten
hen
den
men

PAGE 99
d   h   m   b
jug
rug
tug
dug

PAGE 100
Listen and choose the correct picture.
1. bug
2. jug
3. mug
4. rug
5. dug

PAGE 101
rug
hug
bug
tug
jug

PAGE 102
r   s   c   n
fun
bun
hut
rut

PAGE 103
Listen and choose the correct picture.
1. sun
2. run
3. cut
4. bun
5. nut

PAGE 104
run
fun
hut
sun
rut

PAGE 105
t   s   c   m
rub
cub
pup
bud

PAGE 106
Listen and choose the correct picture.
1. rub
2. tub
3. pup
4. cub
5. mud

PAGE 107
tub
sub
bud
cup
rub

PAGE 108
map
sit
fog
ten
bag
hut

PAGE 109

Listen and choose the correct picture.
1. ill　　　4. up
2. egg　　　5. on
3. add

PAGE 110

mat　　mom　　mud
met　　mill　　mop

PAGE 111

Listen and choose the correct picture.
1. mill　　4. mat
2. mud　　5. men
3. mop

PAGE 112

net　　nut　　nap
nod　　nit　　not

PAGE 113

Listen and choose the correct picture.
1. nit　　4. neck
2. nap　　5. nut
3. nod

PAGE 114

fin　　fog　　fan
fed　　fig　　fun

PAGE 115

Listen and choose the correct picture.
1. fat　　4. fog
2. fin　　5. fan
3. fed

PAGE 116

sat　　sun　　sip
sob　　set　　sad

PAGE 117

Listen and choose the correct picture.
1. set　　4. sad
2. sun　　5. sob
3. sit

PAGE 118

hem　　hut　　hog
ham　　hen　　hop

PAGE 119

Listen and choose the correct picture.
1. hip　　4. hem
2. hit　　5. hen
3. hug

PAGE 120

jug　　jet　　jam
job　　jig　　jog

PAGE 121

Listen and choose the correct picture.
1. Jill　　4. jig
2. jam　　5. jug
3. job

PAGE 122

rug　　rat　　rip
rod　　red　　run

PAGE 123

Listen and choose the correct picture.
1. rip　　4. rug
2. red　　5. rig
3. rod

PAGE 124

log　　lip　　leg
lap　　led　　lot

PAGE 125

Listen and choose the correct picture.
1. log　　4. lap
2. led　　5. lad
3. lip

PAGE 126

bag　　bus　　bed
bib　　bog　　bat

PAGE 127

Listen and choose the correct picture.
1. bed　　4. beg
2. bat　　5. bug
3. big

PAGE 128

pen　　pad　　pop
pup　　pin　　pet

PAGE 129

Listen and choose the correct picture.
1. pet　　4. pup
2. pot　　5. pan
3. pen

PAGE 130

dig　　dam　　den
dip　　dot　　duck

PAGE 131

Listen and choose the correct picture.
1. dad　　4. dug
2. dam　　5. dot
3. dig

PAGE 132

tub　　tag　　top
ten　　tip　　tug

PAGE 133

Listen and choose the correct picture.
1. tag　　4. top
2. ten　　5. tub
3. tot

PAGE 134

get　　gum　　gas
gill　　got　　gap

PAGE 135

Listen and choose the correct picture.
1. get　　4. got
2. gap　　5. gull
3. gill

PAGE 136

cut　　kid　　cod
cat　　cub　　cot

PAGE 137

Listen and choose the correct picture.
1. can　　4. kit
2. cub　　5. cut
3. cot

PAGE 138

nut
pen
hat
dig
tub
cut

PAGE 139

t	p		p	t
n	t		t	n
b	s		s	b
p	n		n	p
m	g		g	m
p	t		t	p

PAGE 140

cat
hut
bug
tap
wet
wig

PAGE 141

run
hen
hop
fog
sit
tub

PAGE 142

hat　　　　bug
hit　　　　bag
hot　　　　big

nut　　　　pop
hut　　　　mop
hug　　　　map

PAGE 144

red　　　　brown
green　　　pink
blue　　　　black

gray　　　　square
yellow　　　circle
white　　　　triangle

PAGE 145

black　　　circle
green　　　oval
pink　　　　rectangle
red　　　　square

PAGE 146

pencil　　　globe
hat　　　　skirt
book　　　　doll

crayon　　　yo-yo
cap　　　　chair
desk　　　　shirt

PAGE 147

book　　　　cap
desk　　　　coat
doll　　　　dress
yo-yo　　　hat

PAGE 148

egg　　　　lemon
nut　　　　corn
pea　　　　rice

milk　　　　cheese
apple　　　meat
ham　　　　cake

PAGE 149

boot　　　　cake
cap　　　　fig
coat　　　　ham
hat　　　　pea

PAGE 150

mop　　pig　　jet
run　　bag　　pot
ten　　sun　　map

PAGE 151

Listen and choose the correct picture.
1. log
2. hen
3. rat
4. bed
5. fog

154

WORKBOOK ACTIVITY INSTRUCTIONS KEY

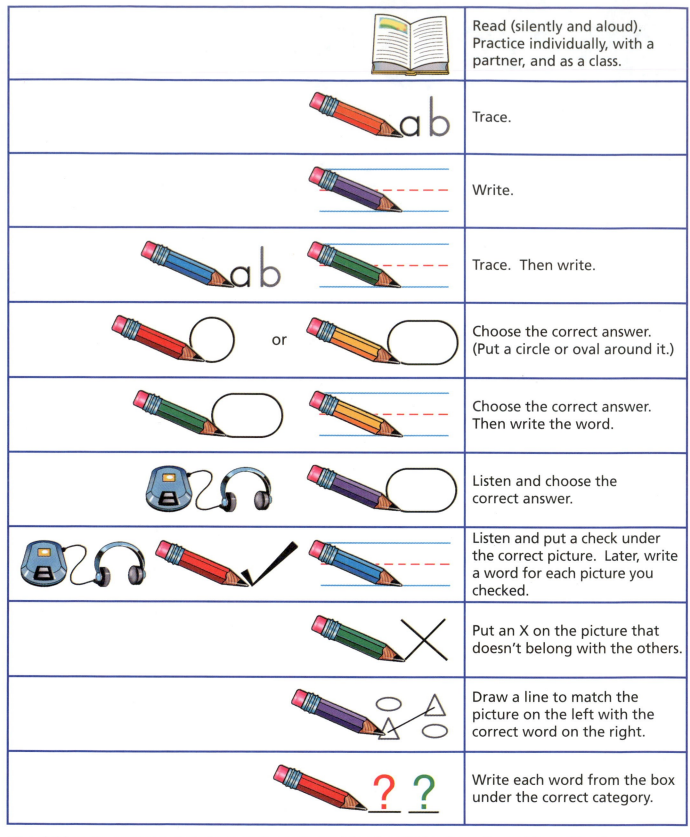

	Read (silently and aloud). Practice individually, with a partner, and as a class.
	Trace.
	Write.
	Trace. Then write.
	Choose the correct answer. (Put a circle or oval around it.)
	Choose the correct answer. Then write the word.
	Listen and choose the correct answer.
	Listen and put a check under the correct picture. Later, write a word for each picture you checked.
	Put an X on the picture that doesn't belong with the others.
	Draw a line to match the picture on the left with the correct word on the right.
	Write each word from the box under the correct category.

Give children the opportunity to hear and say all words in all activities throughout this workbook. Children can do the activities silently in school or at home and then practice saying the words aloud as a class, with another child, or with a tutor, aide, parent, or other adult.